If There Were No LUTHERANS...

...Would There Still Be GREEN JELL-O?®

Life One Sign at a Time

By Rev. Steve Molin

©TUNDRA FILMS®
Marine on St. Croix, MN 55047

If there were no LUTHERANS....would there still be GREEN JELL-O®?

Published by Tundra Films, Inc., P.O. Box 205, Marine on St. Croix, MN 55047. (651) 433-4499.

First Printing: May 2005
Second Printing: October 2005

ISBN# 0-9767875-0-4

Visit our website at www.ChurchSignGuy.com.

Edited by Jim Maher
Designed by Tom Maakestad/Mark Odegard
Photography by Tomy O'Brien

Dedicated to:

The members of
Our Savior's Lutheran Church
Stillwater, Minnesota

*Your love for me, for God and for one another
is the best Church Sign I have ever seen!*

INTRODUCTION

We've all seen them; church signs with moveable-type letters that proclaim a brief message of hope or a timely invitation to worship. That's what our church sign was supposed to be when it was installed four years ago. But then a funny thing happened! Actually, a funny sign happened!

I was going on vacation, so I put up a sign that read:

**Now is a good time to visit.
Our pastor is on vacation!**

When I returned the next week, I changed the sign to read:

Shhhh! He's back!

The response was positive...and immediate! "Hey, here's a church that can poke a little fun at itself." Over the next few weeks, I continued this self-deprecating perspective, along with taking a few good-humored shots at other circumstances and current events. People loved the signs...and *The Church Sign Guy* was born!

The sign has put us on the map in our community, and the 8,800 cars that pass by daily still find words of wit, and warmth, and humor that changes two to three times per week. Often, as I'm changing the sign, passersby will honk, or wave, or give me the "thumbs up" sign. (In fairness, that's not the only gesture they use).

In these pages, you are about to read some of my favorites, chosen from the nearly 300 sayings that have been displayed over four years. Each has appeared on our sign in Stillwater, Minnesota. Most are original, but where I borrowed an idea, I tried to acknowledge the source. I sincerely hope I omitted nobody.

One afternoon, I received a call from a spirited, creatively gifted filmmaker by the name of Gayle Knutson, asking if she could do a short film on the sign. It never occurred to me that this project was film-worthy, but then, I had never met a spirited, creatively gifted filmmaker before! Gayle has created a documentary about these signs and the smiles that have been brought to the faces of our neighbors and friends. So sit back, grab a bowl of popcorn or a bowl of Jell-O®, and enjoy the book *and* the show!

Steve Molin

Church Sign Guy –
The Good Humor Man

At times, those of us who support a church community take our jobs and ourselves a bit too seriously. Our signs can lighten things up. If I can give the people driving by a good chuckle, it makes their day a little bit better. And if the sign hits the right nerve (call it marketing!), maybe they'll look inside the church, too.

JOHN THE BAPTIST AND BILLY THE KID

have the same middle name

Got weeds?
Let us spray

*I first saw this in a newspaper headline
and it seemed fitting for us.*

What's another word for THESAURUS?

PLEASE DON'T WOK YOUR DOG ON CHURCH PROPERTY

SO THERE WAS THIS DYSLEXIC ATHEIST WHO DIDN'T BELIEVE IN DOG

BAKERS WHO LIVE IN GLASS HOUSES SHOULDN'T THROW SCONES

What's the best time to visit the dentist? 2:30? Yes!

Tooth-hurty. . .get it?

Lord, Give us patience. Right now!!!!

A common refrain that, ironically, has stood the test of time.

Will Rogers never met Sign Guy

*Kids, ask your parents
(or maybe your grandparents)
if you don't get this.*

Sign Guy on Atkins
(For sale - 350 boxes of Girl Scout Cookies)

NICE
Four-Letter Words
Snow, Golf
Love & Piza!

I admit it . . . I ran out of nice four-letter words.

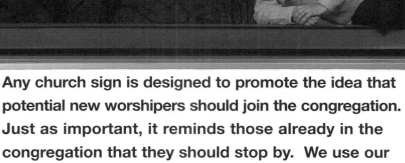

Get To Church!

Any church sign is designed to promote the idea that potential new worshipers should join the congregation. Just as important, it reminds those already in the congregation that they should stop by. We use our church sign to this effect – but in a way that is a bit outside of what you normally see.

Got Soup?

Just another way of promoting the Lenten custom of serving soup and bread suppers on Wednesday nights. Yes, we serve milk too!

Communion Sunday
1,000,000 Served

Now is a good time to visit.
Our pastor's on vacation!

Then, the following week....

Shhhh!
He's back

Plenty of front row seats still available

Don't come to church Sunday
(Come Thursday)

A way to promote our summer Thursday evening outdoor worship service. One parishoner didn't get it....and sent a chilly note to the Church Sign Guy.

Olive Street...
Olive Branch....
Peace to Olive you!

Yes, our church is located on Olive Street.
How could we resist?

Something's missing in our CH—CH

U.R.

A favorite old saw of many churches.

We're calling our new addition "The West Wing"

OUR NEW WEST PARKING LOT IS NOW OPEN (NO ZAMBONIS PLEASE)

Hockey fans (like me) will understand.

IN ETERNITY ONLY THREE THINGS MATTER: LOCATION, LOCATION, LOCATION

WELCOME TO SEA WORLD: THE PORPOISE-DRIVEN LIFE

Every time we mess up Jesus gets Cross with us

CAN'T SLEEP?
WE CAN HELP.
OUR PASTOR'S
SERMONS
ARE AVAILABLE
ON TAPE!

ZZZZZZ

Pastor saw his shadow. Six more weeks of lousy sermons

You're not lost. You're right there!

A sign obviously written for men who want to avoid asking for directions

You a sinner?
There's always room for one more.
Join us!

Hey! We've got just one word for people like you! (welcome)

LIVE GRACIOUSLY.
YOU MAY BE THE ONLY SERMON SOME PEOPLE EVER READ

In the News

Today's headlines, whether dealing with politics or some of the other major issues of the day, provide endless fodder for one-liners on our sign. So why leave all of the fun to the folks at the Daily Show?

Join Us for Worship this Sunday

(Mr. Smith & Mr. Wesson, Not Invited)

Our state had just enacted a law allowing people to conceal and carry guns. This is our version of the often-seen sign "we ban guns on the premises."

Support Stem Sell Research: Buy Flowers!

SENATE TALKS 40 HOURS, BREAKS OUR PASTOR'S RECORD

|||| |||| |||| ||||
|||| |||| |||| ||||

SIGN GUY FOR SENATE

Talk about Instant Messaging – this went up the day after an incumbant U.S. Senator announced he wouldn't seek re-election.

If the Electoral College had a football team, who would they play?

It's Over!
And the mail carriers
are very happy!

Our post-election farewell to political junk mail.

DON'T GO TO MARS TO LOOK FOR LIFE - WORSHIP WITH US

Now offering Anger Management Class for cows

Remember Mad Cow disease?

Read my lips -
No more pretzels

The first President Bush had a signature line about "no new taxes." His son the President had an unfortunate choking accident with pretzels.

If the Electoral College had a basketball team, would they play on the Supreme Court?

An idea from a member of our church staff

IF YOU SEE BLACK SMOKE RISING FROM OUR CHURCH, PLEASE CALL FIRE DEPT.

This appeared the same week the College of Cardinals was sequestered to elect a new Pope - not that anybody would confuse our church with the Sistine Chapel.

The Sports Page

Sports is a universal language - except of course for the millions of you who could care less about sports. Today, the sports stories that go beyond the scores create easy targets for humorous signs.

"I do a sign when I want to do a sign."
THE SIGN GUY

My tribute to moody NFL star Randy Moss, quoted as saying "I play when I want to play."

A lot of Olympians have gone downhill

HOCKEY IN HEAVEN?
THERE IS NOW!
(Thanks, Herbie!)

In our hockey-crazy state, we fondly remember Herb Brooks, who coached the "Miracle on Ice" U.S. Olympic hockey team to a gold medal in 1980. He died in a car crash in 2003.

PACKER FANS. COUNSELING AVAILABLE HERE

A note to our neighbors from Wisconsin who happen to drive by after a bad Sunday for their home team.

HOCKEY IS MENTIONED IN THE BIBLE:
"Esau loved the Wild game."

Credit this to the mayor of St. Paul, home of the Minnesota Wild of the National Hockey League.

BASEBALL IS MENTIONED IN THE BIBLE:
"In the big inning"

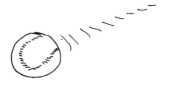

Yankees or Twins? Let's debate

The sign we posted the day the New York Yankee-Minnesota Twin playoff game was scheduled opposite a televised Presidential debate.

Fishing or golf? Let's de-bait

"I ADMIT IT, I BET ON CHURCH LEAGUE SOFTBALL"
Sign Guy

After Pete Rose finally admitted to betting on baseball games.

Jesus: Kinder than an Olympics gymnastics judge

ARE YOU WATCHING THE MASTERS? THE MASTER'S WATCHING YOU

There's more to life than golf.

THE SUPER BOWL: COMMERCIALS, INTERRUPTED BY A FOOTBALL GAME

Talking About The Weather

One of the joys of living in Minnesota is that we get a taste of all four seasons. Sometimes, it is more like a huge bite. But whether it be rain, sleet, snow or humidity, it is all worthy of some comment from the Church Sign Guy.

Hey Noah, still got those blueprints?

We're a river town, and every few years, the water rises over its banks.

Prayers for snow not allowed until November 15

Too hot to change the sign

Hell is hotter than this,
but it's a dry heat

Rain, Snow, Sleet, Hail: It's Still Water

A play on our hometown, Stillwater, Minnesota.

Haven't seen the Son in awhile? Join us Sunday

"FOR MANY ARE COLD, BUT FEW ARE FROZEN."

Matt 22:14

DID YOU ENJOY THE WARM WEATHER? JUST TEASING!
- God

After an unseasonably warm winter week, reality returned.

Ski Nebraska

Praying for a blizzard?
Go to Dairy Queen

*Both signs came in the middle of a
snow-less winter in Minnesota.*

AUGUST

A gust of wind
Oh, yeah, our
Pastor's back!

The Good Book

Like anybody in my position, I take the bible seriously. But who says God can't inspire a sense of humor? Sometimes, the people and events noted in scripture open the door to messages that I hope generate laughter of biblical proportions.

MOSES WAS A BASKET CASE IN DENIAL

Looking for the Shepherd?
The Shepherd is looking for ewe

When did Cain kill
his brother?
As soon as he
was Abel

There's a reason they're not called "The 10 Suggestions!"

Feeling old?
Noah built the ark when
he was 500 years old.
Enjoy your youth

The God of love is smiling down on you today.
SMILE BACK!

What did Adam say to Eve?
I'll wear the plants
in the family!

Kids count too

Kids are the center of our lives, but are also too easily overlooked. I like to use the sign from time to time to remind folks that our children are our future. They deserve every moment of attention we can share.

Children should be seen and not hurt

1. Hug your kids
2. Pray for your kids
3. Repeat steps 1 and 2

Please drive carefully; Those backpacks have little kids attached to them!

A reminder on the first day of school.

Holiday Time

Holidays are a big deal in the church. Christmas and Easter are the most important, of course, and we like to take advantage of these special days to create messages that speak to the time of year.

Have you ever watched a turkey dressing?

"Sing Choir's of Angels"
(OK, so they're just people)
Cantata this Sunday

Christmas - Easter. Why not stop in between the holidays

A message to our CEOs (people who attend church on Christmas and Easter Only).

Grass...The River...Jesus All Have Risen

Just our way of saying "Happy Easter!"

What's a four-letter word for springtime?
(See other side)

Lent

If you're not thankful you must be a turkey!

Tired of fowl?
Come to the fair!
Advent fair Sunday 5 p.m.

*With apologies to Shakespeare
("fair is foul and foul is fair.")*

It's a boy!
Merry Christmas!

FOR SALE:
Two Front Teeth.
Free Giftwrapping

Planning to worship on Christmas Eve? Dress Rehearsal Sunday

It's not a costume. I have a cold and I'm a little horse

A sly play at Halloween, which Lutherans don't officially recognize.

This shall be a sign for you - a baby lying in a manger

Do New Year's Resolutions carry any weight?

God's Love is not Lent, It's Given

The Joys of Lutheran-hood

Lutherans have earned a reputation as being a rather quiet and understated group. But I say why not shout out and celebrate! We're proud of our faith and our heritage. The sign gives us a way to show the world that Lutherans are a humorous breed as well.

LUTEFISK:
The Piece of Cod Which Passeth Understanding

This is a Lutheran Scandanavian favorite.

If there were no Lutherans...would there still be Green JELL-O®?

Three things Lutherans love-
Lent, Advent, Thrivent

Guess which one of these is not a religious season, but a financial services company for Lutherans.

Lutherans are most dense in Minnesota

The good ideas of others

It is fun to be creative with the signs. And then there are those days when it is nice to just take advantage of somebody else's creativity, or fame and borrow (at least a little) from what's already out there.

Father, Son and the Holy Spirit: Get to know 'em!

Borrowed from a slogan for the Minnesota Twins baseball team. (Thanks to my daughter-in-law)

Martin Luther Live – (Well, sorta)

Really, just me in costume.

We're changing our name to Dayton's

The longtime Minnesota department store chain, Dayton's, dropped its flagship name after being acquired by another company. Why not capitalize on their brand?

Now Serving Krispy Kreme Communion Wafers

Your life on a Rocky Road? You should try Sundae School

Happy Meal : $2.49
BMW: $55,995
God's Love: Priceless!

Local flavor

Stillwater, Minnesota, our home, is a beautiful city on the banks of the St. Croix River, bordering Wisconsin. It was a lumber mill town. Those days are long gone, but we have celebrations such as Lumberjack Days. Of course, we also take pride in our Minnesota connections and our rivalry with Wisconsin.

Message to Lumberjacks: Seek, Knock & Axe

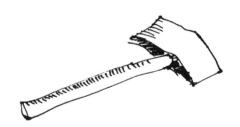

Hey Wisconsin! What a friend we have in Cheeses

Credit this to a Lutheran assembly held in Wisconsin, where I first saw this sign posted.

Lumberjacks are just people with an axe to grind

Are you a little board?
Thank a Lumberjack!

Have you "thawed" about visiting the Ice Palace

St. Paul's Winter Carnival features a huge castle that eventually melts.

Sermon on a stick

The perfect pitch at Minnesota State Fair time, where you can get everything from hot dogs to deep fried pickles on a stick.

About the sign

The sign at Our Savior's Lutheran Church has taken on a life of its own. Thousands of cars roll by every day. Because of its now legendary status, the sign itself, along with the Church Sign Guy, are easy pickings for a few jabs.

Sign guy fired - Job opening

Sign broken: come inside for message this week

Submitted by a member of our youth group.

Dear Local Admirer,
Answers to questions:
1. Yes   2. No
-Sign Guy

A guy named Sam loves our signs

It pays to compliment the Church Sign Guy. Sam, a stranger, stopped by earlier to praise the signs.

Whatever job you do, you should always plan ah ead

There's only so much space on each line of the sign.

Those two dips in the road are not our pastors!

A popular sign during road construction in front of our church.

Looking for a sign
God loves you?
Okay, God loves you!

My name is Sign Guy and I approve this message

Sign Guy Gone - Your Ad Here

If you like our sign, you'll love our church

And that's the bottom line.

If There Were No LUTHERANS....
...Would There Still Be GREEN JELL-O®?

A great gift!
A perfect fundraising tool!

Any Lutheran you know (and even those who aren't Lutheran) will love this book and laugh out loud at the documentary DVD. **"If There Were No LUTHERANS...Would There Still Be GREEN JELL-O®?"** Use the form on the opposite page to order additional copies.

Raise Money
This warmly irreverent and inspirational book/DVD is perfect for church fundraising activities or to sell all year round. Order in quantity at a discount and use "If there were no LUTHERANS . . ." to give a financial boost to many church projects. Use the form on page 140 for bulk fundraising orders.

Clip and return the order form with your check or credit card information to: Tundra Films Inc., P.O. Box 205, Marine on St. Croix, MN 55047. Call (651)-433-4499 or order on the Internet at **www.churchsignguy.com**

Order More Copies for Yourself, Family and Friends

If There Were No LUTHERANS....
Would There Still Be GREEN JELL-O®?

Name _____

Address _____

City, State, Zip _____

Check enclosed ☐   VISA ☐   MasterCard ☐   DISCOVER ☐

Credit Card # _____ Expires _____

$14.95 per copy plus $2.00 shipping/handling **per book**

of copies ordered _____ x Price per book $ _____ = Total $ _____
+ Shipping per book $ 2.00 x # of copies _____ = Total $ _____

Subtotal = $ _____

Minnesota residents only add 6.5% sales tax   + MN sales tax = $ _____

TOTAL = $ _____

Or order online at ChurchSignGuy.com

Order Bulk Quantities for Fundraising

If There Were No LUTHERANS....
Would There Still Be GREEN JELL-O®?

Name _____

Church _____

Address _____

City, State, Zip _____

Check enclosed ☐   VISA ☐   MasterCard ☐   DISCOVER ☐

Credit Card # _____ Expires _____

Order 25 or more copies $9.00 each (40% discount) with FREE SHIPPING

# of copies ordered _____ x Price per book $ 9.00 = Total $ _____

Send to: Tundra Films®, P.O. Box 205, Marine on St. Croix, MN 55047
Or order through our Web Site www.ChurchSignGuy.com